TIPS

Music Activities in Early Childhood

Compiled by
John M. Feierabend

Hartt School of Music
University of Hartford
West Hartford, Connecticut

Music Educators National Conference

Table of Contents

Foreword

The Music Educators National Conference (MENC) has created the TIPS series to provide music educators with a variety of ideas on a wide range of practical subjects. Each TIPS booklet is a compilation of methods, ideas, and suggestions that have been successful in the music classroom. MENC has designed this quick-reference series to be used as a starting point for creating and adapting projects for your particular situation.

TIPS: Music Activities in Early Childhood is designed for music educators who are involved in teaching children from infancy to kindergarten.

Finding the Head Voice

As young children begin to speak, they imitate the sounds they hear. If they hear only spoken language, they will imitate that language but may not make vocal sounds that go beyond the tessitura of normal speech in their language. In addition to emphasizing spoken language, adults working with young children should make many sounds using the higher range of the voice. Tell stories that include talking animals, speaking with high, medium, and low sounds. (For example, read the part of Baby Bear in "The Three Bears" with a very high voice).

Tell the same stories over and over until the children begin to imitate you. Then, each time a character's name is mentioned, pause and have the children perform the appropriate sound. The same idea could be used in a story about everyday sounds in the home, outside, at school, in the woods, and so forth.

* * *

Help children notice all their voices. Whisper "Little Miss Muffit." Then experiment: say it in a talking voice, in a singing voice (improvising a melody), and in a very high or very low voice.

* * *

Chant a nursery rhyme like "Jack and Jill" using the following arrangement of words: Jack and Jill went up up up up up up up the hill to fetch a pail of water." As you chant the word up, let your voice go higher and higher. At the end of the rhyme, pretend to cry, using a very high voice, and say something like "Poor Jack hurt his head."

* * *

Young children often sing in a speaking voice or a "chest voice." Playful games can be used to help these children expand their vocal ability into their singing voice or "head voice" ranges. With a slide whistle or a siren whistle (perhaps borrowed from the band director), demonstrate a variety of sliding sounds and ask the children to imitate those sounds with their voices.

* * *

Ask the children to sing on a neutral syllable and, while they do so, tell them to take a small bunch of their own hair and make believe they are puppets on a "string." At a signal, children lift the "string" and stand on tiptoe while simultaneously inflecting their voices upward. Generally, this throws them into their head voices.

* * *

1

Play a game in which each child stoops as low to the floor as possible. At a given signal, children slowly rise, "sirening" their voices higher and higher as they get into a standing position. The "winner" is the one who can produce the highest pitch.

After "practicing" vocal sirens in imitation of the teacher's voice, a string glissando, or a slide whistle, children love to follow, with their siren voices, the path of a filmy scarf tossed in the air and permitted to float down. Vocal sounds stop as soon as the scarf settles to the floor. The scarf can also be waved through the air while children imagine the sounds their voices will make in imitation; then, they can actually imitate the movement with their vocal sirens.

* * *

Read the children a story about animals. Pause and have the children create each of the animal sounds as you are reading.

* * *

Have the children pretend to be your "mountain echo." Have one child stand across the room from you. Cup your hands and sing short melodic patterns on *so* and *mi*. The child should echo whatever you sing. "Yoo hoo" (*so–mi*) is a good starting point for the echo game.

* * *

Use puppets to demonstrate high and low sounds. Have the children help you tell stories or chant rhymes using their high, middle, or low voice. (A good source book is Helen Wyzga's *Simple Gifts, Book I*).

* * *

Play echo games: Say "this is my whispering (speaking, calling, singing) voice." Then, have the children choose from the four vocal statements and echo you, performing one on their own.

Alternately, speak single words or short phrases with extreme vocal inflections. Invite the children to echo you. Consider using a child's name: "Let's say Mary's name with our very low voice." Have the children practice repeating the name using high, sliding, and singing voices.

* * *

Sing songs that have short echo patterns in them. Have one child sing the pattern as a solo, using a play microphone as a prop. One song to use would be "There's Someone Living on a Big High Hill" from Deanna Hoermann's cassette recording *Catch a Little Song*.

* * *

Young children can make high-pitched "train whistles" before and after singing songs about trains. When the sound is expected to be very high, it often puts the child's voice in the head register. The peer pressure of sounding like a group of train whistles helps, too.

* * *

Children enjoy the "funny" feeling of speaking in their singing (head) voices. Using two puppets to signal each of the two voices, cue the children's use of both voices in alternation. First, the children speak an entire chant (for example, Silverstein's "The Sitter" from *A Light in the Attic*) in one voice or the other. Then the puppet for the opposite voice is shown for the second half of the chant, and eventually phrases are chanted in alternating voices. Gradually, individual children demonstrate their mastery of the register switch, choosing which puppet they will begin with and alternating from there. Great fun! The singing-voice puppet can also be used as a reminder to the children to use the appropriate register when singing songs.

* * *

Pattern Matching Games

Inviting children to take turns matching patterns does much for the development of the musical mind/voice connection. Nonthreatening games are the best way of evoking responses from the children. Barbara Andress has designed a wooden microphone (available from the World of Peripole) that is used to show children whose turn it is to sing. The teacher can quickly go around a circle of children, asking each child to sing a fragment of the echo song into the microphone. A percussion mallet or even a paper-towel tube can substitute for a microphone just as well. Singing traditional echo songs such as "My Aunt Came Back," "Oh My, No More Pie," or "Bill Grogan's Goat" are ideal for evoking solo singing into the "microphone."

* * *

Play a game where children are seated with eyes closed. Roll a ball to a child while singing on any simple pitch pattern, "Ball, ball, who has the ball?" The child who has the ball answers on the same pattern, "Me, me, I have the ball." A second child tries to identify who has the ball only from hearing the first child's voice. The child who guesses correctly gets to roll the ball on the next turn as the game continues in a similar fashion.

* * *

Using a bean bag, a yarn ball, a play microphone, or something similar, sing a greeting to each child. The pattern could be the same for each child or could incorporate a variety of tone sets. For example:

	s	l	s	m
You sing	"Hel-	lo	Mar-	gie"

	s	l	s	m
The child sings	"Hel-	lo	Teach-	er"

	s f	m r	d	d
You sing	"Hel-	lo	John-	ny"

4

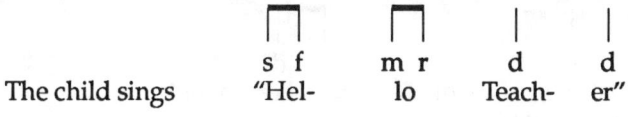

The child sings   "Hel-   lo   Teach-   er"

* * *

Play "Fill in the Blank" games. Sing phrases of songs, leaving out the last beat or beats of the phrase. Using a play microphone, select soloists to fill in the blanks with the appropriate word, pitch, and rhythm. Use, for example, "Down Came a Lady" from Peter Erdei's *150 American Songs to Sing*.

* * *

Roll a Nerf ball to a child while asking questions such as "What's your favorite animal (ice cream, vegetable)?" sung with a simple melodic pattern. The child responds to the question with the same melodic pattern. Initially, *so–mi* can be used, and later other pentatonic patterns can be tried. The children eagerly await the opportunity to receive and roll the ball and to sing their favorite animal, toy, season, and so forth.

* * *

Ask interesting questions of the children. For example:

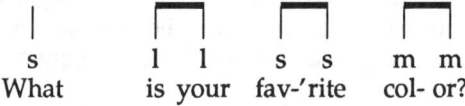

s   l l   s s   m m
What   is your   fav-'rite col- or?

Ask them to answer your questions with similar sounds. They might answer with something such as:

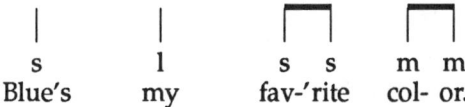

s   l   s s   m m
Blue's   my   fav-'rite col- or.

Other appropriate questions include: Who is your friend? Who is your favorite teacher? What is your favorite toy? What will you be on Halloween?

* * *

Play guessing games with the children. They enjoy stumping you, and you in turn achieve your goal of setting up an opportunity to match pitch. For example, tell a child to think of a number from one to ten.

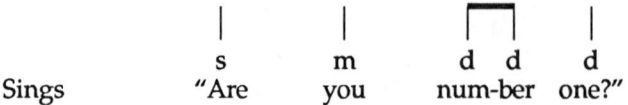

Sings   "Are   you   num-ber   one?"

The child might answer, to the same melodic pattern, "No, I'm number five." Ask the child to pretend he or she is a farm animal.

Sings   "Are   you a   cow?_____

The child should use the same melody to answer something such as "No, I'm a horse." Keep score, and be sure everyone gets a turn.

* * *

Using a puppet with a workable mouth, have the child and/or class match melodic patterns given by the "puppet." After matching, children enjoy anticipating a big kiss from the puppet! This is especially useful to encourage individual singing among three- to five-year-olds.

* * *

Allow children to explore playing a drum with mallets during free play time. As a child plays a rhythm pattern that can be imitated, repeat the pattern on another drum. The child will notice the "game" that he or she has begun and will delight in trying other patterns for you to imitate.

* * *

Teaching New Songs

There are many ways in which children can learn new songs. Some songs are best learned simply by being "caught," while others require more careful listening through rote repetition. The ultimate goal is to have the class be able to sing a song without your assistance. Sometimes it is necessary for you to sing a song many times for the class before inviting them to sing. Having the children perform some motions while you sing the song will keep them involved while they hear the song repeated several times.

* * *

An effective way to teach a song is to show a series of pictures representing the words of various phrases of the song. As you sing the song, place the pictures on the floor in front of the circle of children. These pictures serve as visual reminders of the song's words. Accordingly, if each phrase is represented by a picture, the children are also visually and orally learning the form of the song as they sing it.

* * *

When opening the class with a sung greeting, use a folk song. For example, sing the following words to "Skip to My Lou": "Hello, Jimmy, how are you, Hello Sarah, how are you, Hello Mary, how are you, How are you today?" Continue until all of the children's names have been included. In addition to serving as a greeting, this technique helps the children begin to learn the melody of the song itself.

* * *

Help children become conscious of the sounds they sing by providing them with a beginning pitch before they start to sing. Hum the first sound of a song; then, on that sound, sing words such as "Let's begin 'Old MacDonald' on this sound. Can you make your voice sing this sound?"

* * *

Sometimes introducing a song hummed through a kazoo or played on bells is effective since the children are taken with the different sound and may pay closer attention to the tune itself. Immediately after playing the song, sing it to the children and ask them to join in.

* * *

Children learn songs by *hearing* them. Find ways to repeat the same song many times, on several different days. Do not expect the children to sing the song at first: if you do, you may inhibit their learning because they have not heard the song frequently enough to sing it correctly. Let them absorb it through their ears. When a child has heard the song enough, he or she will sing it.

* * *

The best way for young children to learn new songs is to add movement, pantomime, or actions of some kind. This involves the whole child and aids in memorization and learning.

* * *

Many folk songs can be acted out. When teaching a song such as "A Hunting We Will Go," invite the children to pretend to go hunting around the room with you. Pretend to catch a fox and put him in a box and then let him go. Think of ways to act out other folk songs. Children love the activity and will want to sing the song over and over. They may be so busy acting out the song that they do not sing the song, but they are hearing it as you sing. Thus, they are prepared to sing the song later.

* * *

Play a game with a new song. After many repetitions, begin to mouth the words and pantomime the actions to encourage independence on the part of the children. For example, while mouthing the words to "Star light, Star bright," pass a wishing star around the circle to the beat of the song:

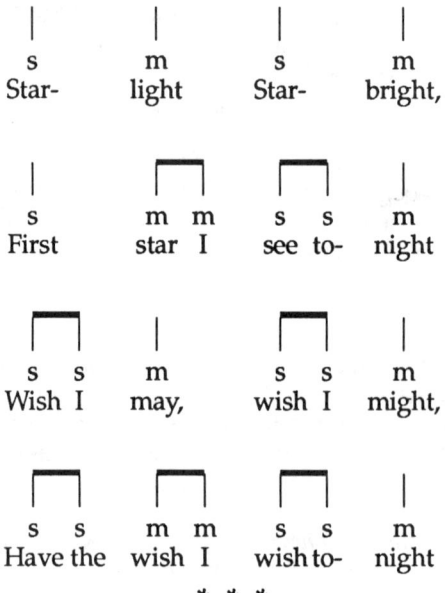

s	m	s	m
Star-	light	Star-	bright,

s	m m	s s	m
First	star I	see to-	night

s s	m	s s	m
Wish I	may,	wish I	might,

s s	m m	s s	m
Have the	wish I	wish to-	night

* * *

8

Children love to play with flannel-board figures. Allow children to manipulate animals on the flannel board for songs such as "The Farmer in the Dell" and "Old MacDonald."

* * *

Before teaching a new song, look at its inherent qualities. Use these qualities as a basis for asking questions about the song. Ask enough questions so that the children will have reason to listen several times and stay actively on task. For example:

- Ask questions regarding the story or text.
- Ask questions regarding the rhythmic or melodic form (if simple enough).
- Discover how many phrases are in the song.
- Count beats.

* * *

Instead of always teaching songs from beginning to end, sometimes teaching songs from end to beginning can be very effective and can add variety to rote teaching procedures. Even more important, this procedure sets the children up to feel very successful because they feel a pride of accomplishment each time they complete something, even if they didn't do it all by themselves.

After singing the complete song for the children, teach them to sing the last logical musical unit of the song (depending on the song, this may be a complete phrase or only the last few words). Next, sing the song from the beginning, cueing the children to join in and finish. Then teach them the next to the last musical unit to add to the last one, and again have them join in at the appropriate time, continuing to string the chain backward until they are singing the whole song. Because listening repeatedly to the first phrase is built into the process, these phrases will be familiar and easy to learn by the time you arrive there.

This procedure works particularly well for songs that do not have a lot of repetition or that have distinctive endings. For example: Try this with "Pumpkin Pumpkin" from *The Song Garden*, starting with the "just like that" ending, then completing the last phrase, "turn into a jack-o-lantern just like that." Finally, add the whole first phrase, with which the students are familiar by now, to complete the song: "Pumpkin, pumpkin, round and fat/ Turn into a jack-o-lantern just like that!"

* * *

An occasional alternative to rote repetition involves introducing songs previously used for creative movement as new singing songs. Although this requires foresight and planning, the song is already familiar to the child when introducing the lyrics, the tune, and so forth. Visual aids always help children remember lyrics; for example, you can make small puppets with Popsicle sticks or fabric to dramatize a song's story. "Perform" the song for the class, and later let the children take turns with the puppets. Likewise, folk-song picture books, such as *London Bridge* illustrated by Peter Spier or *Twinkle Twinkle Little Star* illustrated by Jannat Messenger, are fun ways to teach new songs.

* * *

Creative Movement

During the preschool years, movement activities can do much for the development of the child's psychomotor skills and creative expression. The movement themes of Rudolf Laban can serve as a guide to exploring a variety of movement effects. Those "themes" include awareness of body parts and the whole body, weight and time, space, flow, and partners and groups.

* * *

There are so many possible creative movement activities! One that my preschoolers enjoy is the singing of "Sally Go Round the Sun." On "BOOM!" they must freeze as scary statues (as scary as possible without making a sound!). They can also be goofy statues, happy statues, or sad statues. A variation of this activity is to have them move around the circle in a scary, sneaky, goofy, sad, or happy way while singing the song, then freeze in the same mood of statue on "BOOM!":

s	s	s	s	l	s	
Sal-	ly	go	round	the	sun;	

s	m	m	s	s	m	
Sal-	ly	go	round	the	moon;	

s	s	s	s	l	s	m	d
Sal-	ly	go	round	the	chim-	ney	pot

m	m	r	r	d	
Ev-'	ry	af-	ter-	noon	BOOM!

* * *

Invite children to explore "light and gentle" movements using the following fantasy. Have each child imagine he or she is floating inside a large bubble. Have children gently nudge their bubble from one side of the room to the other, being careful not to break it. "The Fishes" from *Carnival of the Animals* by Saint Saëns is nice background music for this activity.

* * *

Have the children perform the following pantomime: Blow up a balloon, fasten the balloon with a string, parade around the room with the balloon being careful not to bump into any other children, let the balloon soar high into the sky, pull the balloon down toward you, and, finally, on the count of three, pop your balloon.

* * *

To help children learn to work with others, have them scatter and freeze around the room. When all are still, the teacher plays two, three, four, or five times on an instrument such as the triangle, slowly and purposefully. The children quickly and quietly form groups of that number and join hands. Play a short melody, familiar or improvised, and have the children improvise a dance together. Repeat the activity. Each time vary the mood of the melody. ("Reet's Game" from Hermann Regner's *Music for Children: Volume II*).

* * *

Help children discover their individual body parts and their whole body by singing such songs as "The Wiggle Song: from *Music for Little People* by John Feierabend or "They're a Part of Me" from *Piggyback Songs for Infants and Toddlers* by Jean Warren.

* * *

Young children have a rich form of imagery that they apply to music and how music moves—but it is an imagery that is visual and kinesthetic rather than verbal. The most imaginative dancing from prekindergarten children can be nurtured by teacher-prepared audiotapes designed to elicit spontaneous dance to short examples of music. To prepare the tape, select four to six instrumental musical examples of contrasting styles. Tape a thirty-second to one-minute excerpt for each style (including a moment of silence between each example). To introduce the music to the children, let them listen first while seated. Next, tell them that they will hear some music from far away and long ago (or from present times). Ask them to imagine how people move when they dance to this music. Invite them to "see" the people as they listen. Then, prepare a space for moving, and instruct the children in the proper *traffic rules* for dancing. Instruct them to listen for the music to stop. When the music stops, they stop; when the music starts again, they move again. The inventive teacher can prepare a variety of tapes and encourage spontaneous dancing with young children as a regular part of their musical experiences. Their musical expressiveness, guided by the music, may surprise you.

For this activity, try *Dances of the World* from the Nonesuch Explorer Series and selections ranging from baroque dances to bluegrass fiddle tunes, and from jazz, big band and new age music to the sound track from an Indiana Jones movie. These provide a rich stimulus for music dancing and young children. (Hint: try dancing to these musical selections yourself before you take them to the classroom.)

* * *

The foundation of music appreciation is built during the early years. Great music should be a part of the environment of every child. Play a recording of something by Bach, Beethoven, Mozart, or any of the great masters. Rock with a very young child as the music plays, or take his or her arms and swing with the beat. "Dance" with the child to the music, moving fast if the music is fast or slowly if the music is slow. Help the child move various body parts to the music (for example, make his or her fingers, elbows, or eyelashes dance).

* * *

Following the Child's Preferred Tempo

Children are often able to maintain a beat at a consistent tempo if allowed to initiate the repeated movement at a tempo that is comfortable for them. Once a child has begun the repeated movement the teacher and class can support that movement by singing a song using the demonstrated tempo. Choose a song such as "Did You Ever See a Lassie" and ask the leader to show the motion he will use before the class begins singing. This allows the child to establish a comfortable tempo.

* * *

When singing a familiar song such as "Twinkle, Twinkle Little Star" or "Twinkle, Twinkle Christmas Tree" have a child "bounce" a paper star or Christmas tree in the air to indicate the preferred tempo. Have the other children all sing and follow the child's bouncing object.

* * *

The same philosophy would hold true when a child accompanies a song on an instrument such as tambourine, rhythm sticks, triangle, bells, or Autoharp (supply the chord changes and have the student perform the strum). Ask the child to play first, and then have the song match the tempo of the child's playing. Because each child has his or her own inner tempo, it is better to have only one child play at a time if your goal is to have the children keep a steady beat. You might then ask the class how one student's performance was different from another's. Words like faster or slower and louder or softer can be used for comparison. You might even want to ask the children which tempo best fits the song. Prekindergarten children must have an opportunity to sense and do.

Musically play with the nursery rhyme chant "Jack Be Nimble." Help children sense the underlying pulse of the chant and add a voice inflection challenge to the game, as follows:

Prepare a tapping page chart to be placed on the wall at the child's eye level. (See the accompanying illustration.) The youngster plays the page by using his or her finger to tap the pictures of Jack while chanting the rhyme. The game continues by the finger tracing the line up and over the candle stick while the voice makes the appropriate low-high-low sounds (ooooh) to express the big jump. A loud spoken "KA-BOOM," accompanied by a tap on each stage of Jack's unfortunate landing, ends the game.

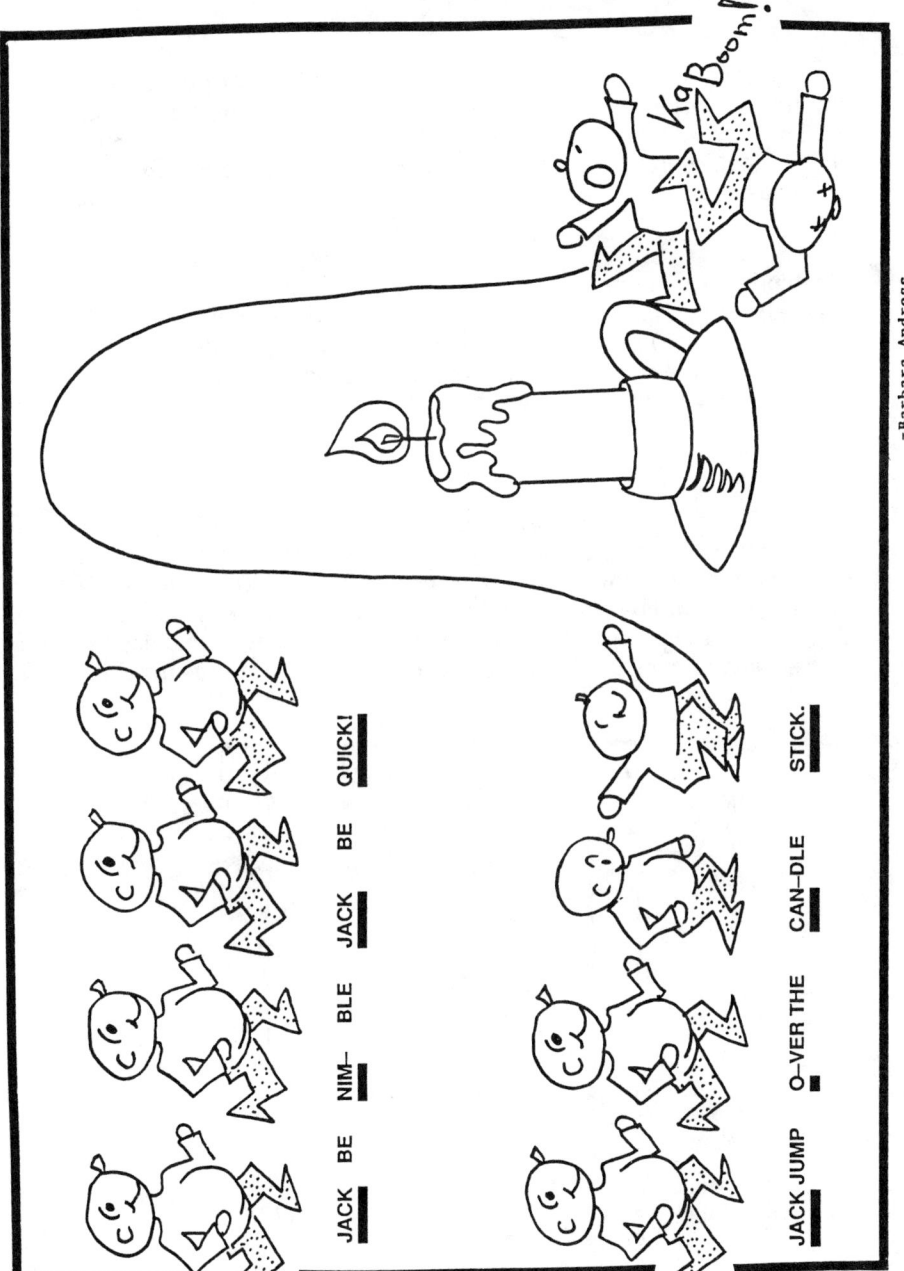

JACK BE NIM–BLE JACK BE QUICK!

JACK JUMP O–VER THE CAN–DLE STICK.

KaBoom!

–Barbara Andress

Dynamics Games

Many songs or rhymes include dynamic variation. For preschool children, experiencing various dynamic levels is more important than learning "about" dynamics. To help children experience these levels, sing a lullaby softer and softer while pretending a stuffed animal is falling asleep.

* * *

Pretend you are marching in a band in a parade. Play a Sousa march. As the band gets closer to town, turn up the volume on the record player. As the parade leaves town, turn the volume down on the record player. Teach the children a marching song. Have the children sing louder as they march into town and softer as they travel out of town.

* * *

Using the folk song "Lucy Locket," play a dynamics game. All children sit in a circle (Lucy's purse hidden underneath one of them). One child, who is "it," tries to discover who has the purse. Clues are given by the children by singing louder when "it" is closer to the person who has the purse and by singing softer when "it" moves away from the person with the purse. "It" has three guesses to discover who has the purse. Never let the loud singing get "chesty" or raucous as the children sing:

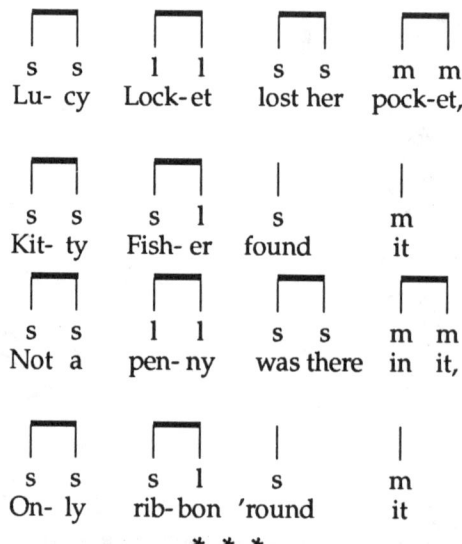

s s	l l	s s	m m
Lu- cy	Lock- et	lost her	pock-et,

s s	s l	s	m
Kit- ty	Fish- er	found	it

s s	l l	s s	m m
Not a	pen- ny	was there	in it,

s s	s l	s	m
On- ly	rib-bon	'round	it

* * *

16

Say the chant "Engine, Engine" many different ways:
- Pretend the train is outside the classroom (loud).
- Pretend the train is in the next town (soft).
- Pretend the train is traveling from another town to your classroom (getting louder).
- Pretend the train is leaving your room and traveling to the next town (getting softer).

* * *

Tempo Games

Some songs are intended to be sung at various speeds. "Do Your Ears Hang Low" is a favorite old fingerplay. Each time the song is sung, go faster and faster while performing the motions, so the children experience how tempo can change.

* * *

Tempo changes can be explored with rhymes such as "Engine Engine Number Nine." The rhythm can be chanted as if the train is just getting started in the morning (slow) and gradually gains speed. The train can be rolling downhill at a good speed and then encounter a mountain that it must climb (fast to slow). Then introduce combinations of uphill and downhill motion. You can use a model train prop and a model hill. As you position the train on the slope, the children chant the appropriate tempo.

* * *

Some songs suggest a change in tempo from verse to refrain ("Rig A Jig Jig" from *Musical Games, Fingerplays and Rhythmic Activities for Early Childhood* by Wirth and Stassevitch); or from verse to verse ("Jim A Long Josie" from the same book).

* * *

Take known songs and ask the children to sing them at various tempos. Discuss which tempo is the most appropriate for each song.

* * *

Timbre Games

Play a game where one child sits in the center of a circle with eyes closed. Another child chants the first child's name. The child in the circle must then decide who is calling based on the timbre of the voice he or she hears.

* * *

After children have had the opportunity to hear and play many instruments, play a listening game. Instruct the children that you will be playing one of three instruments in front of you. Let the children see the instruments but not hear their sounds. Review the names of the instruments. Have the children close their eyes. As you play the instrument, the children should pantomime how the instrument is played. (First be sure that the three instruments are quite different in timbre.) You will be able to assess from the pantomime motions that children are correct (assuming the procedures for playing the three instruments are all different). The children then open their eyes, watch you play once again, and name the instrument.

* * *

Blindfold one child. Pass two, three, or four different simple rhythm instruments out to other children in the class. The instruments should have clearly distinct timbres (for example, tambourine, finger cymbals, wood blocks, cow bell) and be instruments that the children have played many times before, so that they are familiar with the sounds produced. A song is sung with the entire class tapping the beat. Then, the two, three, or four children with instruments play the beat on their instrument—one instrument for each phrase of the song (the other instrumentalists stay quiet while each instrument is featured). Point to each child as he or she is about to play. At the end of the song, the blindfolded child must indicate which instrument was first and which was last. If the child is very adept at this, he or she should tell you what was played on the second and third phrases when four instruments are used. Naturally, in the beginning, only two instruments would be used.

* * *

Place five sound sources (such as a drum, triangle, maraca, jingle bell, and woodblock) in a row in front of the children. Hide five matching sounds in a box. Play one of the sounds and ask a child to choose a sound that matches the one you played.

* * *

Using a tape recorder, have children create an aural Halloween collage, each contributing a Halloween "sound" (for example, the cackle of a witch, the hoot of an owl, the meow of the black cat, or the spooky sound of a ghost). Play the tape for the children and ask them to raise their hands when they hear their own special Halloween sound.

* * *

Help children notice the sounds around them by drawing their attention to sounds throughout the day. As they prepare to go out and play, ask them to close their eyes and then listen to determine what is happening outside. (They may hear sounds such as birds chirping, the wind blowing, other children playing, or trucks or cars.) Have a "listening time" every day. At that time, all other activity stops and everybody listens. Ask them, "What do you hear today?"

* * *

Sharing the Beat with Infants and Toddlers

In many cultures babies are brought to adult musical ceremonies and bounced or rocked on the beat. We can help infants and toddlers acquire an understanding of beat by gently tapping on them while listening to music. Try playing "Pat a Cake" by tapping on the child's open palms while speaking the rhyme. Later hold your hands under the child's open palms (but do not tap) and speak the rhyme. Often the infant or toddler will supply "what's missing" and begin to tap on your hands. Adjust the tempo of the rhyme to match the child's tapping.

* * *

Dance with your child while singing or listening to music. The child can be held in your arms or the child may rock back and forth on his or her legs.

* * *

When children are bouncing in their beds, rocking on their horses, tapping on their high chairs, jumping in Johnny Jump Ups, or swinging on swings, sing songs that fit the mood and tempo of the activity.

* * *

Many children love to clap their hands together. Add songs such as "Clap, Clap, Clap Your Hands," "If You're Happy and You Know It, Clap Your Hands," and "Pease Porridge Hot" to your child's clapping. Adjust the tempo to match the speed of the child's clapping.

* * *

Managing Groups

Generally, it is desirable to communicate in music class with less talk and more music. For example, children are often required to stand up and sit down several times in the course of a lesson: A musical way of cueing the class is to use a soprano glockenspiel. Pulling the mallet across the glockenspiel from low to high signals the class to stand; from high to low signals the class to sit.

* * *

Sing simple theme songs whose texts tell children to stand, sit, or move to a new location. For example, use the tune "Skip to My Lou" and change the words to something like "Everybody stand" (sit, march to the door). A clean-up song can signal children to put things away; it may be as simple as "Time to put your toys away, Time to put your toys away, Quickly as you can" sung to *so* and *mi*.

You could also use a song such as "Go Tell Aunt Rhody" as a command song. Change the words to fit the direction needed: "Go get your coat on, Go get your coat on, Go get your coat on, and line up by the door" or "Let's make a circle, Let's make a circle, Let's make a circle, and then we'll clap our hands."

* * *

Choose a greeting song and a good-bye song from music books and use those same songs every day to greet and to say good-bye to the children. The repetition will ensure that the children learn the songs and will provide a daily routine, which is important for little children.

* * *

When a child is not supposed to peek, use the directive "close and cover" (close eyes and cover closed eyes with hands) to help ensure the desired result. No guarantees, of course!

* * *

Instruments can be distributed without frustration. For example, children enjoy walking "like grown-ups" to the basket of rhythm sticks and taking their pair. Then they can follow the directive to "try out your sticks to be sure you have a good pair" and, after they have practiced a bit, to "form a teepee with them on the floor." The entire procedure takes a few seconds, the children are allowed to follow their natural urge to make sound, and you never need to say, "I don't want to hear them until it's time to play."

* * *

To promote positive participation during class, a "Biwilloby Bag" works wonders! This bag contains something special and different each day, but the object inside can only be discovered if the class follows directions and participates. It may contain a new song, an instrument, a puppet, a folk-song picture book, or a favorite circle game. Not only does this help you be creative with the contents of the bag, but children love the "surprise"!

* * *

Young children are much more likely to become restless and to misbehave during instruction time, such as listening to a teacher talking, than when they are engaged in music activities. Even when attempting to keep talking to a minimum, however, there are things that must be said and instructions that must be given. By *singing* the words rather than speaking them, you can impose structure on this verbal material, turning it into a musical event. Using just a few pitches and simple rhythms, recitative style, you create a musical framework that will increase the likelihood that student attention will be obtained and maintained.

* * *

Developing Community Interest

The benefits of music play in the preschool years are well documented. Somehow inspiration needs to be given to those who spend their days with preschoolers—parents, day-care workers, and nursery school teachers. One school offers a once-a-month meeting called "Parents as Teachers." Music in early childhood has been a favorite topic at these meetings and has been presented every year for the past several years. Parents in the community are contacted and invited to attend the meeting, during which lectures and demonstrations are given to share activities that can help prepare the child for school. Parents are delighted to learn a few songs, rhymes, and activities in which they can musically play with their children at home.

* * *

More music educators should be encouraged to start preschool music classes at their local churches or synagogues, schools, and colleges.

* * *

Music educators should inform parents in their schools of the recent research regarding music for the young and offer suggestions to parents in the form of workshops or parent-teacher organization presentations.

* * *

Encourage college students majoring in elementary education or music education to visit, observe, and assist classes in preschool music. Invite music educators to serve as guest lecturers to college students majoring in music education or elementary education.

* * *

Suggest that local music stores set aside a section for song collections and recordings for prekindergarten children. Encourage them to explore what is available for the young so that they will have a wide selection on hand. They might have a list of suggested masterwork selections for home listening.

* * *

One college conducts a "Family Fun 'n Frolic Day" once a semester for parents, grandparents, relatives, and friends of preschoolers enrolled in college-sponsored "Music for Children" classes. Games, dances, and musical activities are enjoyed by all. The two-hour activity ends with a potluck lunch for all.

* * *

"Reading Days for Children," held by many libraries, provide a ready-made opportunity for preschool music teachers to volunteer to "sing a story" during story time. Interest is high when the teacher taps the beat on each page of a book while singing the story. Many illustrated folk-song books are available for this purpose.

* * *

List of Resources Cited

Andress, Barbara. Wooden microphone. The World of Peripole, Inc. Brown Hills, NJ 08015-0146.

Dances of the World. Nonesuch Explorer Series. Electra/Asylum/Nonesuch Records Compact Disc 979167-2

Erdei, Peter. *150 American Songs to Sing.* New York: Boosey and Hawkes, 1985.

Feierabend, John. *Music for Little People.* New York: Boosey and Hawkes, 1989.

Heath, Carol. *The Song Garden.* Books 1–3. West Hartford, CT: Kodály Musical Training Institute, 1984.

Hoermann, Deanna. *Catch a Little Song.* Manitowoc, WI: Silver Lake College, n.d. Cassette tape.

Messenger, Jannat. *Twinkle Twinkle Little Star.* New York: Macmillan, 1989.

Regner, Hermann. *Music for Children: Volume II, American Edition.* New York: Schott, 1977.

Silverstein, Shel. *A Light in the Attic.* New York: Harper and Row, 1981.

Spier, Peter. *London Bridge.* Garden City, NY: Doubleday and Company, 1967.

Warren, Jean. *Piggyback Songs for Infants and Toddlers.* Everett, WA: Totline Press, 1985.

Wirth, Marian, and Verna Stassevitch, *Musical Games, Fingerplays and Rhythmic Activities for Early Childhood.* West Nyack, NY: Parker, 1983.

Wyzga, Helen. *Simple Gifts, Books I, II, and III.* Manitowoc, WI: Silver Lake College, 1982.

Acknowledgments

MENC gratefully acknowledges the following educators who contributed to this booklet:

Barbara Andress .... Arizona
John M. Feierabend .... Connecticut
Catherine Jarjisian .... Ohio
Susan H. Kenney .... Utah
Nancie Kester .... California
Danette Littleton .... Tennessee
Wendy L. Sims .... Missouri
Diane Skrobis .... Wisconsin
Jean R. Thomas .... Tennessee
Debbie Walker .... Oklahoma
Sister Lorna Zemke .... Wisconsin